SILENCE,

TESSA B. BLAQUE

Published by Argyle Fox Publishing | argylefoxpublishing.com

ISBN 979-8-89124-031-5 (Paperback)
ISBN 979-8-89124-191-6 (Hardcover)

Cover image by Chris Fowler

Dedication

To the One who called me
before I understood the cost.

To the fire that refined me.
To the silence that strengthened me.
To the obedience that preserved me.

To my husband—
my covering, my partner in faith,
whose steady love and quiet strength
have walked beside me through every season of growth and refinement.

To my children —
the precious gifts God entrusted to my care,
who daily teach me stewardship, patience,
and the sacred weight of influence.
You are my inspiration of becoming greater each day
and not giving up but giving my all.

To my grandchildren—
each of you, and the precious one on the way—
living reminders that God grants us
second chances to love greater,
deeper, and with softer hearts.
You are grace multiplied
and joy renewed.

To my mom, sisters and brother-in-law—
thank you for all of your love, support, and encouragement.
You kept me lifted in times when I felt alone and depleted.

May you walk in truth, stand in courage,
and know the love of Christ that surpasses understanding.

For those who were hidden and did not mistake it for being forgotten.

— *T.B.B.*

CONTENTS

FOREWORD

It is a real honor for me to write this foreword for Tessa B. Blaque's poetry book.

I have known Tessa not just as a writer, but as my sister-in-law for more than twenty-two years. Over that time, I have seen the kind of woman she is: a dedicated wife, a loving mother, a proud grandmother, a caring auntie, and above all, a kind and genuine person. Those qualities are not just part of her life, but they are also part of her writing. You can feel them in these poems.

What makes Tessa's poetry special is that it comes from a real place. These are not just words put together to sound nice. They come from a heart that has loved deeply, cared faithfully, and paid attention to life in a meaningful way. That is what gives this collection its warmth and sincerity.

Tessa is the kind of person who brings love and kindness into the lives of others, and that same spirit comes through in her poetry. There is tenderness here, but also strength. There is reflection, honesty, and the kind of feeling that only comes from someone who has truly lived and truly cared. Her words are thoughtful without trying too hard, and heartfelt without being forced.

As someone who has known her for many years, I can say that what you find in these poems is true to who she is. Tessa does not have to pretend to be warm, loving, or thoughtful. That is simply who she has always been. The beauty of this book is that it lets the reader see some of that same heart on these pages.

Readers will find poems here that may stir memories, touch emotions, and cause them to reflect on their own lives. That is one of the gifts of poetry, and Tessa offers that gift with grace. Her writing invites you to slow down, to feel, and to think about the moments in life that matter most.

This collection is more than a book of poems. It is a reflection of the woman who wrote it. It carries her love, her gentleness, her strength, and her heart. For those of us who know Tessa, that will come as no surprise. For those meeting her through these poems, I believe you will come away knowing you have encountered something genuine.

It is my privilege to introduce this work and to commend it to every reader. I hope these poems bless you, encourage you, and stay with you long after you have turned the final page.

Enjoy,

Merrill Niswonger

INTRODUCTION

THE PURPOSE OF MY STORY

Have you ever felt that you didn't fit in or belong because of how someone made you feel? Have you ever been made to feel unpretty, undervalued, overlooked and overshadowed? It could have been race, weight, appearance, or personality that made you feel you were experiencing mistreatment or judgment. Truth is, you are absolutely beautiful! We are all fearfully and wonderfully made by God who made us each in His supreme likeness to have uniqueness and beauty that brings Him glory and honor. We should be celebrating our differences! That is what makes us beautiful! We should be giving correction to the ignorance that judges and produces hate and discord. In this book I wanted to highlight racism, systemic racism, bigotry and hate. I also wanted to highlight the beauty within the Black community that has always been seen in a unfavorable light. The Black Culture should be celebrated and appreciated for our contributions and attributes. America has become comfortable with covering up truth and tolerating lies, racism and prejudices. America has given a platform for hatred and racism to resonate instead of causing it to dissipate. In order for growth and change to take place, America needs to hear the ugly truth of the disparagement , division and hardships it has caused people of color. Hatred and racism is in the inner core of America and flows through the bloodlines. America needs to repent after admission and accountability to allow recompense.

Being a black woman, I've experienced racism on so many levels and in many different ways. I have experienced racial discrimination and judgment from multiple races. I have experienced colorism in my own race as well. The truth is that we are one race! We all make up the human race. We have been divided like puzzle pieces that may or not fit when placed in certain areas. We have been separated by color and distinction.

My experiences served as inspiration for a collection of poetry written for those who still believe in the beauty of us all. I wanted to express how I feel through my experience being Black in America. I also want to show there is purpose in pain. Allowing God to turn my pain into purpose helped me to admire the beauty in my tears. It has revealed my strength and capabilities. It also gave me an outlet to express my pain through creativity and spoken word.

God turned my discomfort into confidence and determination to complete my book. Essentially, I didn't know how God would use my experiences until I gave it all over to Him. It was no easy task, but it was a labor of love. Instead of turning my trials into hate, God saw the need to turn them into triumphs. Each triumph is a testament to what God can do with us all if we choose love over hate.

This poetry book aims to redefine how we see beauty. Our beauty isn't defined by the color of our skin. Real beauty is found in who we are as human beings and how we love. Love is a choice. You can choose to love and how you love. I choose to love everyone while loving myself and the skin that I am in. Writing this art piece was enlightening and powerful. I hope you enjoy reading these poems as much as I did composing them.

SILENCE,

my pen
is writing
Blaque
Graffiti

Tell Me Why

Feelin' like a prisoner in my skin,
Innocence shattered and ripped from within.
Accosted by the generational lies of many men
I just can't win. Losing,
My hands are up, I'm calmly speaking,
But they don't hear me 'cause there is shooting!
Lawd, look what we become!
We are dropping like flies!
Target practice is today's pastime.
It ain't no truth in their atrocious lies.
Everyday another life,
Blood-soaked streets with alibis.
Why must another mother cry?
Explain to me why we have to die?
Laws and reforms don't stand a chance
Man's heart is so unstable in hatred that it can't stand.
Weak in morals and values that comprehension can't advance
The minds of the wicked who are paralyzed in a trance.
Stolen memories of time in history but not charged with the crime.
How much do you value your life since you have put a price on mine?

Life Sentence

I was born in a prison
I am currently serving a life sentence
I plead not guilty
My hands are clean but I'm told they are filthy
I fit the description because the depth of my tint
I can't wash it away and all my sins I repent
Don't care to know my name
The system rewards the gain
Another brown girl
Institutionalized with no shame

Made to believe the shackles of incarceration in my mind I am to blame
A figment of my Imagination and fabricated as if I concocted uncomfortable experiences of
interactions.
Exaggeration and lies is what you tell yourself for satisfaction.
Another brown girl mentally and emotionally unstable
Another brown girl, another label.
Ask yourself, does the punishment fit the offenses I didn't commit?
The verdict is in NOT GUILTY
YOU MUST ACQUIT!

I wake up guilty
Get dressed guilty
Drive my car guilty
Go to work guilty
Go to the store guilty
Go to the park guilty
Go to bed guilty
This is my life sentence that I want acquitted.

The Invisible Cage

The invisible cage that nobody wants to admit—
Would you trade places with me and be a part of my life's script?
To deny the bars is to be a part of the systematic depression.
The key to my release is a heart's confession.
To walk a mile in my shoes to you is like being stoned.
Revenge is not what I'm seeking, but equality to be atoned.
My cries go unheard to unlock the cage;
Now as the cage rattles, you are afraid.
The vibration shakes the ground where you stand,
Making cracks in the foundation you built by your hands.
You now realize I have a key, too, that unlocks this cage:
My power and strength.
It's a new day.
We have to change the faces that grip the keys.
We can't move forward until we face the change that will
Set us free.

Tessa B. Blaque

Demonized

Uncivilized
Criticized
Living but not alive
I wake up but the world is still asleep
America has no conscious but aware of those who weep
The stakes are high but my life is cheap
Devalued and underestimated
Not broken but frustrated
The sky has a limit
I'm the most hated
Achievement is an overstatement
Progress just to regress
I'm a criminal no matter how I'm dressed
The spoiled taste of apple pie
Some self-glorified
No one truly sees the pain behind the eyes that cry
Hearts are disguised masking who they really idolize
The root of all evil
Money brings the worst out of most people
The same but not equal

Paper and skin divide neighborhoods
The darker my skin means I'm no good
To make it out means I sold dope
An assumption like I'm shopping but I'm really broke
Change comes when we stay woke
Where there is fire you will see the smoke
Will you help put it out?
Injustice

Color Block

If my pain was a color, there would be no hue
To describe the great affliction I feel
The real disease is in the hearts of those who
Are chosen prey from the first breath
Heavy sighs, a continual silent cry
As the heaviness builds in my chest
As my anger and frustration remain deeply suppressed
Modern-day strange fruit without the lynchin'
The truth of the unseen ropes around our necks that you don't want mentioned
My skin is a quota,
affirmative action or a risk instead of my qualifications, talents, and gifts
Equal-opportunity lenders if your skin has a cool undertone,
Denied a place to call home
Forced to affordable housing in a red zone
Areas of gray designed to keep me down 'cause you realize my future is bright
My skin may be dark but I walk in light
I will fear no evil as I walk through the valley of the shadow of death
The path of struggle that you have prepared for me makes me tired
But won't take my breath
We come from a generation of strength instead of wealth
Battered but not broken
Forgotten but not left
Behind us is the old mentality as we strive in labor
Blessed and truly highly
Favored

Miss Understood

I'm just another jigaboo,
New day, new age,
No makeup, face covering, or mask required for this stage
With no clue, one of many
Picaninny, porch monkey
Nigger woman spellbound
Voodoo
A marked coon no better than dirt
A price was placed on my head from conception to birth
Uncivilized, ghetto, loud rat by way of the hood
I'm just another bitter woman,
Hello, meet Miss Understood
Since you know me better than I know myself
Can you tell me how to attain my mental health?
I feel and carry so much pain that goes untreated
I'm told it's not real on a daily
You would rather my strength be defeated, depleted.
I have more wounds than I have wealth
I could cry a river but I chose to love my . . .

Selfish, liar, labeled whore by my attire
I can dream but with no desire
I'm Miss Understood, trial by fire
Under the impression of hidden aggression
I've suppressed for too long my true confession
I come from an ancestry of great succession
Preceding before me is royalty that goes unmentioned in history lessons
Misconceptions, inaccurate perceptions cause you to assume
I'm society's affliction in contradiction
Reality is, I'm a walking blessing
Assumptions are a form of ignorance when we don't formally greet
I'm sorry your expectations are not for me to meet
Hello, I'm Miss Understood.

Miss Understood:
The Backstory

As a black woman, I've always felt I will never be good enough in society's eyes until a recent epiphany. I can recount times when walking into a room of predominantly white people and being stared down as if I was in the wrong room. I have often been asked by my white counterparts, *May I help you?*, as if I didn't belong there without their permission.

These types of experiences over the years allowed me to see that there was truly nothing wrong with me or my appearance. The problem rests in the heart of those who choose to see my appearance as a threat. Preconceived notions have been evident in my life throughout the years. I walked around with internal wounds that have made me scowl, but that doesn't make me an evil woman. It makes me a human being with real emotions who responds appropriately in a time of need.

As I was writing this poem, I thought of the first time I was called a nigger. I was only five years old, riding my bike along the sidewalk when three white teenagers called me out of my name and spit on me. I didn't know what the word meant and how audacious it was to use it. I do remember how it made me feel and how I responded. I cried out, I'm not a nigger! I didn't know the meaning of the word but I knew it wasn't good. My older three siblings witnessed the atrocity and defended me. I was crying out of fear, and my siblings assured me that it was nothing I did to cause those teenagers to do what they did.

One ignorant encounter does not speak for a whole race or group of people, but it does set the tone. It sets a tone for a person to view a certain race collectively in a negative way because of their experience or belief.

Attention

I don't try to fit in, 'cause I was born to stand out.
I bring water to your mental drought.
I'm not easily persuaded or convinced,
For my eloquent nature won't recompense.
Contrary to your belief, I'm not being overzealous.
The beauty I possess is so magnetic, I don't have to be jealous.
There's no competition:
Permanently in first position,
The atmosphere shifts with my presence.
I understand if I'm not your preference.
I'm not looking to oblige you
Or gain your acceptance.
I am well dressed in elegance and intelligence.
My savory flavor is rooted in the ingredients of my seasoning.
My tongue can be acidic and my lips sweetening.
My traits show I'm a different breed,
Too conspicuous for backgrounds so I take the lead.
The compartment of my mind is where I invest many seeds.
There is no value in renting mental space, now I own the deed.
My substance is solidified by God's influence that gives life to everything I birth.
Every gift I possess is from my Heavenly Father,
Which has been perfected since my existence on earth.
My attitude is not pressed from the stress you try to induce,
Like the spiritual coma you try to place me in using your words to reduce.
But I rise to the occasion
With elation and great anticipation;
For every tear I endured you will have tribulation.
Now that I have your attention,
Your silence is deafening.
I am ENOUGH, and this is the reckoning.

Tessa B. Blaque

Southern Brown Girl

I talk with a southern drawl that is mistaken for ignorance
And I sway with a twist from my confidence but is judged as loose
Too much attitude if I speak my mind and rooted in my truth
My head is adorned in a scarf as my ancestors before me
And my skin is brown kissed from the melanin in my bloodline
The lineage of beauty that flows through my veins is depicted as a disdain
A defect on America's core
My skin remains an eyesore
My beauty is evident but remains unseen
Heart of gold and my worth more than rubies
But diminished to nothing
Very becoming just as the sun rises
I'm viewed as a falling star
I'm told I'm going places but I won't get far
I have grace and abounding potential
This game isn't played as physical but mental
Southern black girl with invisible chains
I walk in freedom but restrictions remain
Southern BROWN Girl
A different day but the judgment and circumstances are the same.

I Am

I am who *I am* not because of my name,
But God created me to be different and not the same.
He created me to be loving, kind and unique.
He designed me with detail,
Passion, and above defeat.
You ask me my name, but it doesn't make a difference.
I am who *I am* because of my skin's pigment.
I'm only beautiful through the eyes of the beholder
The world looks at my complexion and turns a cold shoulder.
The roots are deeper in the trees that are much older
Blood stains remain that can't be washed away by the rain.
I am who *I am*, but I'm told to be numb to the pain,
Told how to feel as if my affliction isn't real.
A figment of my imagination is how some see my experience.
Being black is survival mode not just an appearance.
I am who *I am* not because you made me this way.
I am who *I am* because God will have the last say.

Sorry, Not Sorry

Sorry my hair doesn't compliment your mood.
You judge me by my appearance with the assumptions and let your fear consume.
My skin makes you nervous and my color doesn't meet your approval.
What makes you justified to petition my removal?
I'm not sorry the thought of me succeeding makes you cringe.
Pardon me, but I live my life in color and in my skin.
Sorry, but I'm not sorry because I walk in peace.
Sorry, not sorry that I won't allow you to destroy me.
Sorry, not sorry that I love everyone,
And you can't change my view of the human race.
Sorry, you are the face of hate.

Black Voices

Not trying to be an inferior face,
But a forever race.
Known for our contribution, love, and the ability through inequalities to thrive,
but mostly for our strength because even in chains we rise.
Known for how the bondage was not just a man's act but a spiritual attack,
Carried out by weak-minded souls who wanted power over soil.
To steal a nation and curse a generation
We got freedom papers, but we were already walking in liberation.
Resilience and motivation serves our determination.
We walk in victory and in celebration,
Condemnation with no hesitation
To inhibit the growth of the chosen and favored.
Hijacked dreams and skill for free labor,
Too superhuman to live a life of freedom without supervision.
Changed the word of God to their own religion,
Spoon-fed lies of a better life and a digested vision of hope
Whipped, chained and suited for a rope,
Diminished illusions conceived from confusion
Because our skin matches the description but doesn't depict the American future.
A glimpse of hell seen through malevolent eyes of evil,
Contrived to serve two masters,
Manipulated to believe separate is equal.
Stolen voices carrying faith like ripples in waters,
Chaos in the wind from screams,
Sheer terror and horror
Ripped from the very depths of shaking vocal cords,
Then molded into a tarnished heritage
Succumb to the mayhem and still tamed as savages.
Knowing the weight of your propaganda can impact a bloodline
Of a lineage that was designed to be divine.
Stories told of old and new,
Fictionalized by most and understood by few.
Black Voices

Black Is the New Beautiful

Black **is the new beautiful** in bold print and color like a magazine cover
I'm so confident in my *Black* that my sway can turn haters into lovers.
Its new to you but old to me
My radiance has been on display for the world to see.
No rivalry, no competition
My beauty deserves its own introduction, credits, and honorable mention.
I come from exquisite creations dating many years back
Who were told they were ugly because of their *Black.*
Smooth like sable, my beauty is a masterpiece of art
Uncharted
Handmade by a genius
With ingenuity and potential.
My blueprint was sketched in ink and not pencil
You may try to erase my past as if my ancestors wasn't enslaved
By the years of oppression and *Black* recession, the scars are engraved
My birth date symbolizes a divine experience in alignment with my Heavenly Father,
Adonai.
I'm so comfortable in me, myself, and I.
I revel in my steps as my reputation precedes me.
My melanin was once a strange fruit hanging from a tree.
Appointed, chosen to lead not follow or bend.
I am a legacy not a trend
The depth of my favored garment has many dimensions
Excuse me as I adjust my crown before I forget to mention
I was skillfully planned and made for my ascension
My greatness preexisted beyond comprehension.
My *Black* has surpassed all understanding
Outstanding
My *Black* is Meaningful.
My *Black* is Beautiful.

A Moment in History

On January 6, 2021, the Capitol Building was stormed by President Trump MAGA(Make America Great Again) supporters. Incited by Trump's lies through his speech, fueled by anger and rage, they took to stomping the grounds with the intent to be seen, heard, promote fear and destruction. Watching the coverage of the insurrection of the United States Capitol building upset me. It also saddened me to see where we are as a nation today. Fast forward to the present January 20, 2025, Donald Trump is inaugurated again as President for a second term. As America watched in shame, America also knew what was to come this term. Trump wanted to finish what he started with his first term which was to create racial and spiritual division and possibly a war among races. The plan was never to make America great for all. His plan is to carry out the assignment of the enemy, Satan. The plan is deception . Trump caused division in the Christian community and admitted to not being a Christian himself but yet made claims of how some

of his decisions were Christian based. He caused so much discord and deflected when asked or being made to take accountability for his lies. As America as whole watched history unfold, Trump will be known to be the least qualified President who is a felon to take office twice. He will also be known for his pride, hatred, arrogance and need for greed, control and gain. Scripture tells us in Mark 8:36, "For what does it profit a man to gain the whole world and forfeit his soul."

Foundation/This Old House

Not built on the rock of assurance,
For it is shaky, weak, and weathered from the elements that be.
For this foundation was built on lies and secrecy.
Tear down this house and rebuild!
This foundation has too many cracks from the blood spilled.
The ghosts of the past haunts us still,
The present resembles the past with chills—
It is cold with a story to tell,
The stench of flesh and blood still lingers and dwells.
If these walls could speak,
They would tell the truth
Of the tragedies that took place in each room.
There are windows but no view,
Only of destruction and struggle that has been subdued.

Break of Dawn

Night's breath falls upon us like a shield with no protection.
Holding on to the very thought of your plan,
Frustrations rise and fear sets in from the trials I don't understand.
Hope is the thread keeping me from coming undone.
I know if I cling to it, I will feel the warmth from the Son.
Before darkness comes a warning:
Weeping may endure for a night,
And my joy will come in the morning.
Dawn is breaking and I feel the gentle breeze.
Now I'm certain my soul is at ease.

A Safe Place

My skin makes you uncomfortable
My hair makes you cringe
My voice makes you nervous
My very existence is dinge.
My smile is cunning
And my walk is jive
Your walk is freedom
I RUN to stay alive
My presence makes you scared
But I mean no harm.
I come in peace
But you sound the alarms.
I show myself friendly, but my demeanor is mistaken for mischief or violence
When I speak to appease you,
You'd rather I stay silent.
We walk on common ground, yet you have the advantage
Hate is your open wound, and love is the bandage.
Love should be the surface of the two-way street we walk.
The streets are lining black and brown bodies in chalk.
Your cries of fear echo louder than my dreams.
That one day, I, too, will feel safe
In hopes that in time we can embrace each other's differences
With tenderness reflecting from our faces.

Life

When you are a visionary,
Life offers everything but the fairy
Tales that are not true
Skies are gray and not blue
Brick walls and worn-out shoes
I'm tired yet thirsty so I continue to follow you
I'm trusting you, God, to lead 'cause my vision is blurred
I'm getting hit from every side no matter which way I turn.
I'm feeling the cold sting of life
Disappointments and strife
The ones who say they love you leave fingerprints on the knife.
Trauma to the dome,
Confusion from feeling alone.
I'm certain that God gives us all a vision.
I'm on a mission,
A one-way street, no head-on collision.
Lord, I'm in need of your guidance and your supervision.
It's people who want to see me in a coffin, to drive in the last nail,
Those that don't want to see me succeed.
They feel that the pot is only as big as their greed.
Jesus, please—right now, intervene!
Keep the haters at a distance,
Protect me from both the seen and unseen.
I keep my friends close and enemies closer,
As you fight my battles just so I can keep my composure.
Let the ones who are against me receive exposure.
You give me strength to go on when I want to lie down.
You give me the faith to adjust my crown.
The darkness is overcome by your light.
I'm submissive to you, Lord.
I give you my life.

When You Are Depleted

When you are depleted mentally, physically, emotionally, and spiritually, you aren't capable of being any help to anyone. No one knows what's best for you better than you.

It's okay to say *no* when necessary. Your mental sanity, peace, and health is always important. It should be a priority to make it a precedent in your daily walk. Saying *no* doesn't always mean that you are being selfish. It means that you have everyone's best interest at heart.

When things are done with the wrong intent, there is a greater chance that wrong will come from it. When it is done with the right intent, it will be blessed.

I have heard *no* from God on many occasions. His *no* is always followed by a greater blessing than what I was asking for. God tells us *no* sometimes with a purpose attached to it. At the moment when the answer to a prayer is *no*, we feel that is the end of it. It can even make you feel all is lost and defeated.

I now realize there is a blessing attached to every *no*. The *no* is God's protection and hand moving on my behalf to bless me with what He has for me. I have learned that some of the things I wanted or thought I needed were not in God's plan for me.

God's best allows me to see how truly blessed I am.

Reflection

Lucent as the Son,
I manifest his light.
Connected beyond the distance of the most preeminent human eyesight,
My soul purpose is intertwined by design with El Shaddai, my first love.
Ascending to new heights of unforeseen destinations, I take flight.
Illuminating peace when man's oblivious heart,
sin-filled from the start, is in conflict with flesh;
The real warfare is with the unseen battles of the dark.
Distinctively fabricated for this journey I embark;
I am a reflection,
A walking revelation,
A unique and divine ensemble of art on display,
Beautifully crafted by my Heavenly Father with perfection.
Created in the image of Jesus who died and resurrected, I walk in power.
The flaws I encountered with valor along the way are some of many blessings.
The blemishes of my existence remain reminiscent of the blood stains; I'm far from perfect.
My significance in Christ is essential.
The totality of my experiences is not coincidental.
I am a reflection of what I allow to resonate in my inner being;
I am a light that carries truth and fire by every means,
Realizing my tongue is sharper than any guillotine.
The power in it holds the life and death of a million unseen.
Not by my esteem, but by the morning star that radiates so bright, I am redeemed.

Reflection: The Breakdown

I was inspired by John 15:1–17 to write this poem.

Lucent as the Son,

Jesus Christ is in me as I am in Him also. We are one joined together as one mind, body, and spirit. Christ is seen in and through me. I am a representative of Christ, and my words and actions should constitute that.

Connected beyond the most preeminent human eyesight,

We are connected to God by faith through Jesus Christ. (Hebrews 12:2)

We are connected by faith to Jesus just like a branch is connected to a tree. Everything we need comes from the vine, including our salvation. He is our source of life, nourishment, and being.

My soul purpose is intertwined by design with El Shaddai, my first love.

My soul belongs to God. He has given me purpose in life. He is our creator, and every thread of who we are is in Him also. Our everyday goal should be to do what is pleasing to God and give Him glory. We won't always make the mark, but we press forward to the finish line.

My first love

We love God because He first loved us. (1 John 4:19) There is no one who can or will come before God and our love because He loved me before I loved myself. He is the one who created me and showed me how to love.

Ascending to new heights of an unforeseen destination, I take flight.

Jesus went to the cross for our sins to fulfill the will of His father God so that we have life and life more abundantly. The divine purpose of Jesus's death was to save humanity.

When I answered the call of Jesus and gave my life to him, I knew that I was called to a higher standard. I wanted to diligently serve God and be a vessel. I also knew that the road on this journey will have unexpected turns and detours. The Holy Spirit gave direction and insight, leading me to my purpose.

I take flight.

I trust God no matter what comes my way. I am connected to God by faith, so He is the only one who can hold me when I am about to fall.

Our faith walk is not always a pleasant stroll. On some days, spiritually and physically we get tired, thirsty, hungry, and irritated during our walk. We may endure the stress and strain of finances, relationships, health issues, and more, but we press on.

Illuminating peace

My focus is to be a peacemaker and not a peace breaker. When we are outside of God's will or living without the knowledge of God, our hearts are ignorant to sin. When we become hearers of the word, there is an expectancy to become doers of the word. I remember hearing the saying, To know better is to do better," and how it spoke to my spirit. Having this revelation made me see the world around me so differently. I wanted to have an impact on a broken world that I saw through God's eyes. The impact started with my spiritual walk and the choices I would make from that day forward.

unseen battles of the dark

Ephesians 6:12 states, "For our struggle is not against flesh and blood, but against the rulers, against the authorities, against the powers of this dark world and against the spiritual forces of evil in the heavenly realms."

Further in Ephesians 6, Paul tells us how to put on the full armor of God. Armor is used to protect the body in battle, which is how it is referenced in Ephesians. I wanted to go a little deeper though. Our bodies are a temple, right? That's' what 1 Corinthians 6:19–20 says. "Do you not know that your bodies are temples of the Holy Spirit, who is in you, whom you have received from God? You are not your own; you were bought at a price. Therefore, honor God with your bodies." (KJV)

The temple has to be planned and decisions have to be made before construction takes place. The planning of the temple takes careful consideration. With construction, permits are also needed to move forward with the projected plan to build. God planned for you and has a plan for you. It all starts with a blueprint.

I love the Bible, because it is a blueprint for our lives. Another word for blueprint is *plan* or *print*. A blueprint is a detailed visual representation of how the architect wants a building to look. God is the architect, and the word is the instruction of how to complete the construction of our lives. Jesus left the prints (footprints) to lead us to the construction site and architect, God. Our lives are under construction daily. What is most important to our construction is our foundation and materials being used to build.

A unique and divine ensemble of art on display

Personality, character and characteristics.

My significance in Christ is essential!

Your purpose and direction in life is important to God! You matter!

The power in it holds the life and death of a million unseen

This line refers to how God tells us in Proverbs 18:21 that we have the ability to be influencers of nations with our words. We have the power to speak over generations that will come after us. The tongue has the power to heal or cause destruction. The destruction can be like a domino effect causing a multitude of chaos.

The tongue can also speak blessings or curses. It is a small part of our body that can cause so much pain in other's lives and affect hearts.

Reflection—The Image

When I wrote "Reflection," I thought of how we as Christians are a reflection of Jesus Christ. Our everyday walk and talk should align with the principles and teachings of Jesus Christ and the Holy Word. I can admit that I don't always meet God's expectations of me. That's when the epiphany resonated that we are perfectly imperfect. The beauty of it all is that He still loves us even when we fall.

It took me countless years to get to this place of peace and acceptance in my life. As an adult, I have learned to accept people for who they are and to meet people where they are in their spiritual walk and journey in life. I would often find myself overcompensating. I would also do things that did not align with the Holy Spirit. Just to fit in, I would drink, cuss, and make rude comments. In the past, I would allow words from people to hurt me and shape my thoughts of myself. I would torment myself by trying to meet the expectations of those whose opinions don't matter. Trying to meet the expectations of others can be exhausting, a never-ending cycle of acceptance challenges for approval. It can lead to an unhappy life and failures because you will never meet their expectations or measures.

The War Within

The battle of good and evil
Evident
Prevalent
If my skin does wrong its to be expected
If your skin does wrong, it's justified
Blind eye, heads turned
If my skin does wrong, it's another lesson learned.
Friend at your convenience
Nigger at your disposal
A culture that was never asked how we feel but imposed on.
Black girl magic duplicated, imitated
When it comes to walking in my skin it's overrated
Classic case of bait and switch
Bought in on a dream but
the wrong price was pitched.
My style ,physique and mannerisms are mocked yet admired in secret
This is who I am but to society it's considered indecent.

The Black Experience

Black is ugly
Black is evil
Black is the stain among America's people
Black is wrong
Black is night
Black is the constant struggle and a silent fight
Black is the day when evil had its way
Black is the eyes of the oppression and its masters of today
Black is the heart of the aggressors filled with rage
All because the color black set the stage
Black is the dirty hands blood-stained and dried
Black is the innocents that have died
Black is the souls of the weary who have cried
Black is the feet of the people marching in stride
United is the voice on the rise!
The Black Experience

Black Girl Sparkle

Her brilliance illuminates the path
As others follow the sway of her hips
Her motion causes commotion
with her entrance and when words exit her lips
She is eminent in her own right
She is beauty in any light
Because *she* glistens at every angle
She takes your breathe at first sight
She is savvy and audacious, true boldness
in her flame
Echoes fill the room of everyone
who wants to know her name
She walks to the beat of her own music
because life begins with her
She is a teacher ,cultivator, innovator and creator.
Her worth is more than rubies for she is called
for a great purpose.
She is confident of who *she* is and
God's precious gift which makes most nervous.
Everything about her is intimidating
from her intellect to her smile
She carries the weight of the world on her shoulders
mile for mile
She is strong and resilient determined to succeed
When confronted with stereotypes and lies
of who *she* is not, she believes
In her inner self *she* knows what is truth
and does not boast
For the world is filled with poison
but *she* IS the antidote
As the world spins on its axis of delusion
She perseveres with a vision and brings it to fruition
because *she* knows who holds the plans for her life.
Her life is a daily celebration of excellence
Evident with references *she* should be the preference
When jaded *she* doesn't walk in acceptance
but conquers more territory
For *she* holds the pen that writes her own story!

Tessa B. Blaque

Melanin

Beauty in multiple shades
Melanin so valuable it was demoted to trade
Colors so beautiful it was mimicked and man made
Can't change the color but attempts to fade
Created to copy what had been feared
While demeaning each tone to silence through the years

Brilliance in black
Presence so strong forced to be in the back
History being erased to cover the tracks
Blood trails in generations don't lie, evidence is facts
Year 2025 projects, brick walls and mortar is a set up for a set back

Demons tremble at the fear of progression
Feeding on the ignorant to execute a regression
Using God as a moniker in every profession
To teach the poor, hungry and tired in color a lesson

Expensive suits, Italian loafers, and lies
Selling the American Dream with a slice of pie
Served cold , signed agreement
Snatching souls for your achievement

Melanin in the family trees
Generational secrets but the blood foresees
Truth tellers and story telling
You can burn books but can't stop *melanin!*

The Beauty in Our Ashes

You thought our dreams went up in a blaze,
in the past and presence of your glory days.
Now hidden in plain sight,
your rage burns as we continue to ignite.
You can't stop a vision that is God given,
no matter how many times you light a match.
It will always be blown out by the spirit that is attached!
You can monitor what we do and how we succeed,
but you will never be able to destroy the seed.

You burned down Tulsa, Black Wall Street, still standing.
To get over something is to have an understanding.

Our roots are deep and strong.
No matter the apology, we can't right your wrongs.
Today you may walk around in invisible sheets,
tomorrow will expose all of your dirty deeds.
For every wrong there is a right.
One day death will find you in your night.
Lies of no wars and medals of peace
just to gain oil in the Middle East
World domination is your fixation.
One day you will die in your own corrupt nation.

Stealing from the weak is your sensation.
Weeping and gnashing of teeth is your last destination.

About the Author

Tessa B. Blaque writes from the sacred space where silence meets truth.

Her work is rooted in reflection, resilience, and revelation—transforming quiet moments into bold declarations. With a voice that is both intimate and unflinching, she explores the layered realities of Black identity, honoring its beauty, complexity, and enduring strength.

Through poetry, Tessa gives language to what is often felt but rarely spoken—grief, grace, resistance, and becoming. Her words are not only an expression, but an offering: a place for readers to see themselves, to feel deeply, and to remember their own voices.

Silence, My Pen Is Writing Blaque Graffiti is her declaration that even in the absence of noise, truth still speaks—and it writes.